U.S. Territories
and Possessions

PUERTO RICO ★ **U.S. VIRGIN ISLANDS** ★ **GUAM** ★ **AMERICAN SAMOA**
WAKE, MIDWAY, AND OTHER ISLANDS ★ **MICRONESIA**

By

John F. Grabowski
Patricia A. Grabowski

CHELSEA HOUSE PUBLISHERS
New York   Philadelphia

Produced by James Charlton Associates
New York, New York.

First Printing

1   3   5   7   9   8   6   4   2

Library of Congress Cataloging-in-Publication Data

Grabowski, John F.
  U.S. territories & possessions: American Samoa, Guam, North Mariana Islands, Puerto Rico, U.S.
Virgin Islands / by John Grabowski, Patricia Grabowski.
  p. cm. — (State reports)
  Includes bibliographical references and index.
  Summary: Discusses the geographical, historical, and cultural aspects of American Samoa, Guam,
North Mariana Islands, Puerto Rico, and the U.S. Virgin Islands.
  ISBN 0-7910-1053-8
        0-7910-1400-2 (pbk.)
  1. United States—Territories and possessions—Juvenile literature. [1. United States—Territories
and possessions. 2. American Samoa. 3. Guam. 4. Northern Mariana Islands. 5. Puerto Rico. 6. Virgin
Islands of the United States.] I. Grabowski, Patricia. II. Title. III. Title: U.S. territories and possessions.
IV. Series: Aylesworth, Thomas G. State reports.

F965.G73 1992   91-30781
910'.9171'273—dc20   CIP
                                            AC

 *Contents*

Puerto Rico

U.S. Virgin Islands

Guam

American Samoa

Wake, Midway, and Other Islands

Micronesia

Bibliography 62

Index 63

Puerto Rico

   In the center of the seal of the Commonwealth of Puerto Rico is a lamb, symbolizing St. John, holding a white banner and rests on the Book of Revelation. The lamb also represents peace and brotherhood. The Commonwealth's motto forms a semicircle around the bottom of the seal. The letters "F" and "I" at the top stand for King Ferdinand and Queen Isabella of Spain. Symbols of the kingdom of Spain decorate the border surrounding the seal, which was given to settlers by King Ferdinand in 1511.

Commonwealth Flag

The flag of the Commonwealth of Puerto Rico was designed about 1895 and officially adopted in 1952. A five-pointed, white star in the center of a blue triangle appears to the left of the banner. The rest of the flag consists of five alternating horizontal red and white stripes.

Commonwealth Motto

Joannes Est Nomen Ejus

The Latin motto of Puerto Rico means, "John is his name." It is taken from the New Testament and refers to Saint John the Baptist.

The sun sets over Puerto Rico.

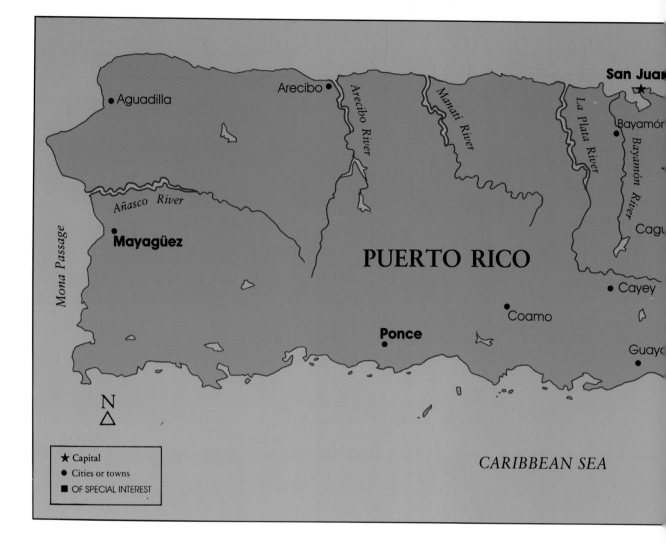

Aguadilla

Arecibo

San Jua

Arecibo River

Manatí River

La Plata River

Bayamór

Bayamón River

Añasco River

Mayagüez

PUERTO RICO

Mona Passage

Cag

Cayey

Coamo

Ponce

Guay

N
△

★ Capital
● Cities or towns
■ OF SPECIAL INTEREST

CARIBBEAN SEA

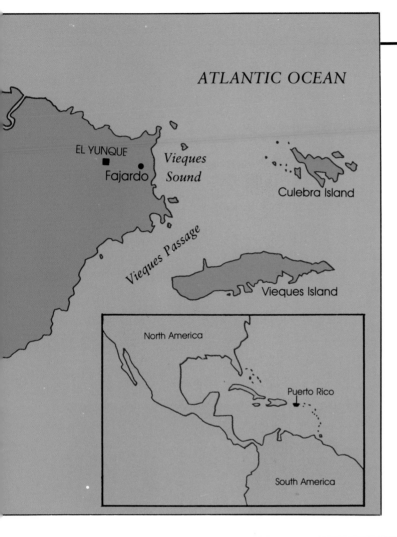

ATLANTIC OCEAN

EL YUNQUE
Fajardo
Vieques Sound

Culebra Island

Vieques Passage

Vieques Island

North America

Puerto Rico

South America

Commonwealth Capital

San Juan has been the capital of Puerto Rico since 1521. Caparra, founded in 1508 by Ponce de León, was the island's first capital. Construction of the present capitol building was begun in 1925. Designed by Rafael Carmoega and built of Georgia marble, it resembles the capitol building in Washington, D.C. The Renaissance-style structure has a large rotunda containing a stained-glass mosaic of Puerto Rico's coat of arms.

San Juan is the capital of Puerto Rico.

Commonwealth Name and Nickname

Puerto Rico was originally called *Borinquen* by the native Arawak Indians. When Christopher Columbus discovered the island on November 19, 1493, he named it San Juan Bautista. The name Puerto Rico, which is Spanish for "rich harbor," originally applied to the capital city. Eventually, the name was used to refer to the entire island. Puerto Rico has also been called the *Island of Enchantment*.

Commonwealth Flower

The maga is the flower of the Commonwealth of Puerto Rico.

Commonwealth Tree

The ceiba, or silk-cotton tree, is the tree of the Commonwealth of Puerto Rico. The silky fiber kapok comes from this large tropical plant.

Commonwealth Bird

The reinita is the bird of the Commonwealth of Puerto Rico.

Commonwealth National Anthem

The national anthem of Puerto Rico is "La Borinqueña," with music by Felix Astol y Artés. Words were later added by Lola Rodríguez de Tío.

Population

The population of Puerto Rico in 1990 was estimated to be 3,336,000. There are 971.2 people per square mile—70.7 percent of the population live in towns and cities. About 99 percent of the people in the commonwealth are of Spanish descent.

Geography and Climate

Bounded by the Atlantic Ocean on the north and the Caribbean Sea on the south, Puerto Rico lies about 1,000

The Camuy Caves of Rio Camuy Cave Park belong to one of the largest subterranean cave networks in this hemisphere.

miles southeast of Florida. The easternmost island of the Greater Antilles, it is 110 miles long, 35 miles wide, and has a total area of 3,435 square miles. The commonwealth includes many small islands, the largest of which are Vieques, Mona, and Culebra. The island of Puerto Rico consists of lowlands along the north and south coasts that rise to foothills further inland. Mountains run across the center of the island, and coastal valleys are found in the east and west. The climate is mild, with an average temperature of 77 degrees. The highest point, at 4,389 feet, is Cerro de Punta, and the lowest point is at sea level along the coast. The major waterways are the Arecibo, Añasco, Bayamón, Blanco, Camuy, Caonillas, Cibuco, Culebrinas, Grande, Guajataca, Guaynabo, Gurabo, La Plata, Loíza, Manatí, Rosario, Toro Negro, Yagüez, Yauco, and Yunes rivers.

Industries

The principal industries of the island are agriculture and tourism. The chief manufactured products are pharmaceuticals, chemicals, metals, electric machinery and equipment, petroleum products, food products, and apparel.

Agriculture

The chief crops of the island are sugarcane, coffee, plantains, bananas, avocados, oranges, yams, taniers, pineapples, pidgeon peas, peppers, pumpkins, coriander, lettuce, and tobacco. Livestock is also important in Puerto Rico; there are estimated to be 579,810 cattle, 210,013 pigs, and 7.4 million chickens and turkeys on its farms. Cement, sand, and gravel are important mineral products. Commercial fishing brings in $7.9 million per year.

Government

Puerto Rico is a commonwealth associated with the United States. The governor, who is elected to a four-year term, appoints other top officials. The legislature, which meets annually, consists of a 27-member senate and a 51-member house of representatives. Senators and representatives serve four-year terms. The most recent constitution was adopted in 1952. Puerto Ricans also elect a resident commissioner, who represents the common-wealth in the U.S. House of Representatives. The resident commissioner may vote in committee, but not on the floor of the House. The people of Puerto Rico are citizens of the United States, but do not vote in national elections. They do vote, however, in national primary elections.

History

Christopher Columbus landed in Puerto Rico on November 19, 1493 during his second voyage to the New World. Although he claimed the island for Spain, no attempt at settlement was made until 1508, when Juan Ponce de León founded Caparra across the bay from present-day San Juan. The Arawak Indians, who inhabited the area, attacked the settlers. Their efforts at ousting the Europeans were unsuccessful, and by the mid-1500s, most of the Indians had been wiped out. Sugarcane had been introduced to the island in 1515, and slaves were imported from Africa to work the plantations three years later.

Over the next several hundred years, Puerto Rico came under attack by Indians from nearby islands, and by the Dutch, English, and French. Spanish colonization continued, however, and after 1850, Puerto Ricans began to yearn for freedom from Spanish rule. In 1897, Spain gave the island a new government that provided for more self-rule.

On April 25, 1898, two

The statue of Ponce de León greets visitors at the San José Church, the second oldest church in the western hemisphere.

months after the U.S. battleship *Maine* was destroyed in Havana, Cuba, the United States declared war on Spain. In July of that year, American troops landed in Puerto Rico. Spain surrendered the island to the United States in the Treaty of Paris, which ended the Spanish-American War on December 10, 1898.

Puerto Rico was governed by the U.S. military until 1900, when Congress set up a civil government according to the terms of the first Organic Act, or Foraker Act. In 1917, the second Organic Act, or Jones Act, made Puerto Rico a territory of the United States and granted U.S. citizenship to its people.

During the early 1940s, a program that became known as "Operation Bootstrap" was started. This effort to improve living conditions on the island included replacing old slum dwellings with modern housing, and improving the educational system. Large farms were divided, and the land was given to farm workers. Many factories were also built.

In 1946, Jesus Toribio Piñero was appointed governor of Puerto Rico by President Harry S. Truman. He was the first native islander to serve in that position. The following year, Congress approved an amendment to the Jones Act that gave Puerto Ricans the right to vote for their own governor. Luis Muñoz Marín became the first elected governor of Puerto Rico and served from 1949 to 1965.

On July 3, 1950, Congress passed a law authorizing Puerto Rico to write its own constitution. On July 25, 1952, the island became a self-governing commonwealth. During the 1950s, thousands of Puerto Ricans migrated to the U.S. mainland in search of jobs and a better way of life. In 1967, the people of Puerto Rico were given the opportunity to become a state or an independent country. They voted to remain a commonwealth.

Today, while farming is still important to the island's economy, manufacturing is the chief source of income. Despite continued industrial growth, unemployment remains high because of the island's large population. Tourism has developed into a multimillion-dollar industry.

Sports

Although cockfighting is a major sport in Puerto Rico, baseball might well be considered the national pastime. There are no professional teams on the major league level, but there is a Caribbean League with a season that runs from October through March. Stadiums are located in the cities of San Juan, Santurce, Ponce, Caguas, Arecibo, and Mayagüez. Basketball is also popular on the island. The Federación Nacional de Baloncesto de Puerto Rico has teams in most of the larger cities. Boxing and wrestling take place throughout the

The trolley takes visitors on a tour of Old San Juan: the city was once enclosed by a wall and protected by fortresses.

year. Popular participant sports include swimming, tennis, golf, and fishing.

Major Cities
  San Juan (population 424,600). Settled in 1521, Puerto Rico's capital is also the island's largest city. The original city, "Old San Juan," is well-preserved and serves as a major tourist attraction. The center of a great, metropolitan area, San Juan is also a popular resort with many beautiful beaches and luxury hotels.
  Things to see in San Juan: Old

San Juan, The Capitol, San Jeronimo Fort (1788), Ponce de León Museum, La Fortaleza, Casa Blanca (1523), Casa del Libro, Museum of the Seas, Capilla del Cristo, City Hall, Botanical Garden, Museum of Fine Arts, Plaza de San José, Casa del Callejón, Casa de los Contrafuertes, Dominican Convent, Plazuela de la Rogativa, Pablo Casals Museum, Plaza de Armas, La Intendencia, Plaza de Colón, San Juan Central Park, Muñoz Marín Park, El Arsenal, San José Church, Museo del Niño, San Juan Museum of Art and History, Pharmacy Museum, San Juan Cathedral, El Cañuelo, El Castillo de San Felipe del Morro, Fort San Cristóbal, San Juan Gate, and the City Walls.

Although the original San Juan Cathedral was destroyed by a hurricane, it was reconstructed in 1540 and stands today as a rare example of medieval architecture in the Americas.

The Ponce Museum of Art houses more than 1,000 paintings and 400 sculptures that range from ancient classical to contemporary art.

Ponce (population 161,700). Located on Puerto Rico's south coast, the island's second largest city is an important commercial port. It is the center of the island's sugar, rum, and textile industries. Nearly 400 buildings throughout the city have been restored, and the wrought-iron balconies, gas lamps, Corinthian columns, and arches are reminiscent of

The Caribbean National Forest, the only tropical forest in the U.S. National Forest System, is usually referred to as El Yunque, named for the mountain in the area.

its Spanish heritage.

Things to see in Ponce: Alcaldía, Plaza del Mercado, El Vígia, Plaza Central, Cathedral of Our Lady of Guadalupe, Parque de Bombas, Toro Negro Forest, Hacienda Buena Vista (1833), Ponce Museum of Art, and Tibes Indian Ceremonial Center.

Places to Visit

The National Park Service maintains one area in Puerto Rico: San Juan National Historic Site.

Near Arecibo: Arecibo Observatory. This observatory is home to the world's largest radio/radar telescope, which is used to study deep-space objects, the planets, and Earth's atmosphere.

Bayamón: Francisco Oller Art and History Museum. This museum is home to a selection of the works of Puerto Rico's greatest artist.

Near Cataño: Barrilito Rum Distillery. A 200-year-old plantation home and 150-year-old windmill stand on the grounds of this rum plant.

Near Fajardo: Caribbean National Forest. Commonly known as El Yunque, the only tropical U.S. national forest receives 240 inches of rain annually.

Near Hatillo: Rio Camuy Cave Park. One of the largest underground river systems in the world runs through the large subterranean cave network of the park, which first opened to the public in 1987.

Loíza Aldea: Church of San Patricio. Constructed in 1645, the church is the oldest continually functioning church on Puerto Rico.

Mayagüez: Mayagüez Zoo. The zoo features more than 340 species of animals from around the world displayed in their natural settings.

La Parguera: Phosphorescent Bay. The waters of this bay shimmer and glow when disturbed, due to the countless microorganisms which live there.

San Germán: Cathedral de Porta Coeli. Built in 1606, the church has been restored as a museum, and houses many religious statues, paintings, mosaics, and ornaments.

Near Utuado: Caguana Indian Ceremonial Park. This restored park was originally constructed by Taíno Indians more than 700 years ago for recreation and worship.

The statute of La Rogativa represents the Spanish Dominion and religion, and it stands near the Governor's Mansion in Old San Juan.

Events

There are many events and organizations that schedule activities of various kinds in the Commonwealth of Puerto Rico. Here are some of them.

Sports: Horse racing at El Comandante Racetrack (San Juan).

Arts and Crafts: Barranquitas Native Handicrafts Fair (Barranquitas), Jayuya Indian Festival (Jayuya), Summer Arts Festival (San Juan), Vieques Cultural Festival (Vieques).

Music: Bomba y Plena Festival (Ponce), San Juan Symphony Orchestra (San Juan), San Juan City Ballet (San Juan), Pablo Casals Festival (San Juan),

Dancers romp through the streets; colorful festivals and musical events make Puerto Rico an exciting place to visit year round.

The Performing Arts Center in Santurce is an elegant building that presents some of the best concerts, plays, and musicals in the Caribbean.

Annual Puerto Rican Music Festival (San Juan).

Entertainment: Flower Festival (Aibonito), Fiesta de Santiago Apostol (Loíza Aldea), Puerto Rican Food Show (Luquillo Beach), San Juan Carnival (San Juan), Tropical Flower Show (San Juan), Le Lo Lai (San Juan), San Juan Bautista Festival (San Juan), Puerto Rico Beauty Pageant (San Juan).

Tours: Bacardi Rum Distillery (Cataño).

Theater: Julia de Burgos Amphitheater (Río Piedras), Drama Festival (San Juan), Puerto Rican Theater Festival (San Juan), Tapia y Rivera Theater (San Juan), Institute of Puerto Rican Culture Theater (San Juan), Performing Arts Center (Santurce).

Famous People

Many famous people were born in Puerto Rico. Here are a few:

Luis Arroyo b. 1927, Penuelas. Baseball pitcher

Herman Badillo b. 1929, Caguas. First U.S. congressman born in Puerto Rico

Carlos Romero Barcelo b. 1952, San Juan. Governor of Puerto Rico

Ramón Emeterio Betances 1827-98, near Cabo Rojo. Physician, writer, and political activist

Julia de Burgos 1914-53, Carolina. Poet

Orlando Cepeda b. 1937, Ponce. Baseball player

Roberto Clemente 1934-72, Carolina. Hall of Fame baseball player

Rafael Hernández Colón b. 1936, Ponce. Governor of Puerto Rico

Angel Cordero b. 1942, San Juan. Jockey

José Cruz b. 1947, Arroyo. Baseball player

Luis A. Ferré was once governor of Puerto Rico.

Justino Díaz b. 1940, San Juan. Opera singer

Pablo Elvira b. 1938, Santurce. Opera singer

Sixto Escobar 1913-79, Barceloneta. Bantamweight boxing champion

José Feliciano b. 1945, Lares. Grammy Award-winning

José Ferrer starred on the stage and screen; he won an Academy Award in 1950 for his performance in Cyrano de Bergerac.

pop singer: *Light My Fire*

Luis A. Ferré b. 1904, Ponce. Governor of Puerto Rico

José Ferrer b. 1912, Santurce. Two-time Tony Award-winning stage actor and Academy Award-winning film actor: *Cyrano de Bergerac, The Shrike*

Ed Figueroa b. 1948, Ciales. Baseball pitcher

Felisa Rincón de Gautier b. 1897, Ceiba. Mayor of San Juan

Guillermo Hernandez b. 1954, Aguada. Baseball pitcher

Raúl Julía b. 1940, San Juan. Stage actor: *The Threepenny Opera, Where's Charley?*

Luis Muñoz Marín 1898-1980, San Juan. First elected governor of Puerto Rico

Felix Millan b. 1943, Yabucoa. Baseball player

Rita Moreno b. 1931, Humacao. Academy Award-winning film actress and Tony Award-winning stage actress: *West*

Side Story, The Ritz
Francisco Oller 1833-1917, Bayamón. Artist
Jesús Toribio Piñero 1897-1952, Carolina. First native-born governor of Puerto Rico
Miguel Piñero b. 1946, Gurabo. Dramatist and actor: *Short Eyes*
Juan Pizarro b. 1937, Santurce. Baseball pitcher
Chi Chi Rodríguez b. 1934, Río Piedras. Champion golfer
Lola Rodríguez de Tío 1843-1924, San Germán. Poet
Antonio Valero 1770-1863, Fajardo. Military officer

Colleges and Universities
  There are many colleges and universities in Puerto Rico. Here are the more prominent,

with their locations, dates of founding, and enrollments.
American University of Puerto Rico, Bayamón, 1963, 4,295
Bayamón Central University, Bayamón, 1961, 2,917
Catholic University of Puerto Rico, Ponce, 1948, 12,507
Electronic Data Processing College of Puerto Rico, Hato Rey, 1968, 992
International American University of Puerto Rico, Aguadilla, 1957, 3,629; *San Germán Campus*, San Germán. 1912, 5,553
Universidad Adventista de las Antillas, Mayagüez, 1957, 788
Universidad Politécnica de Puerto Rico, Hato Rey, 1974, 3,124
University of Puerto Rico at Arecibo, Arecibo, 1967, 3,421; *at Bayamón,*

Bayamón, 1971, 3,849; *at Ponce*, Ponce, 1970, 2,240
Cayey University College, Cayey, 1967, 3,332
Humacao University College, Humacao, 1962, 3,892; *Mayagüez Campus*, Mayagüez, 1911, 9,432; *Medical Sciences Campus*, San Juan, 1950, 2,895; *Río Piedras*, Río Piedras, 1903, 22,210
University of the Sacred Heart, Santurce, 1935, 7,302

Where To Get More Information
Puerto Rico Tourism Company
575 Fifth Avenue
New York, NY 10017
1-212-599-6262 or
1-800-223-6530

U.S. Virgin Islands

The seal of the U.S. Virgin Islands, adopted in 1917, contains the coat of arms of the United States. The American eagle, with its wings outstretched, holds the shield of the United States on its breast and a branch of green laurel and arrows in its talons. The border around the seal reads "Government of the Virgin Islands of the United States."

Territorial Flag

The territorial flag of the U.S. Virgin Islands contains a golden American eagle centered on a white background. The eagle holds the shield of the United States on its breast, a green laurel branch in its right talon, and three arrows in its left talon. The letters "V" and "I" appear on either side of the eagle. The flag was adopted in 1917.

The tranquil blue waters of Cinnamon Bay on the island of St. John beckon bathers from all over the world.

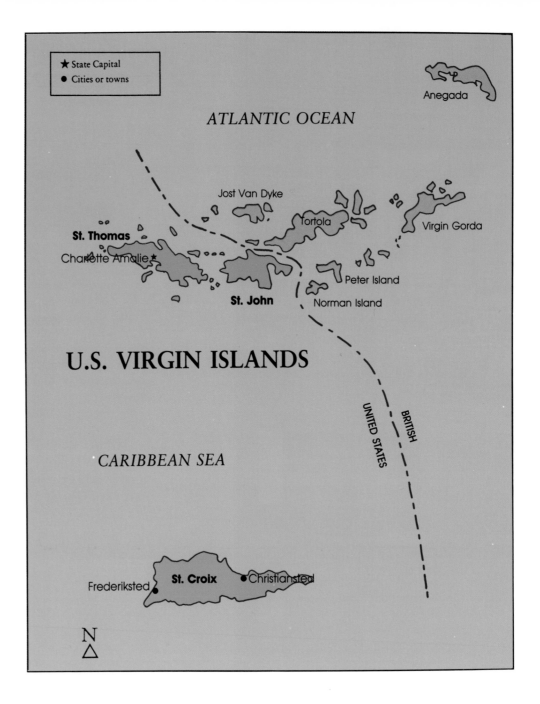

State Capital
● **Cities or towns**

ATLANTIC OCEAN

Anegada

Jost Van Dyke

Tortola

Virgin Gorda

St. Thomas

Charlotte Amalie ★

Peter Island

St. John

Norman Island

U.S. VIRGIN ISLANDS

UNITED STATES

BRITISH

CARIBBEAN SEA

Frederiksted ● St. Croix ● Christiansted

N
△

The Government House in St. Thomas, built in 1747, is a beautiful example of Danish architecture.

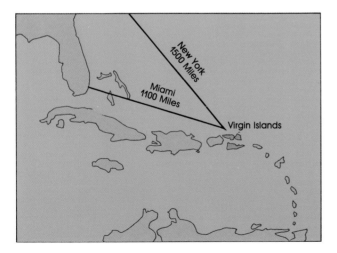

Territorial Capital

Charlotte Amalie, on the island of St. Thomas, was chosen as territorial capital in 1917, when the United States purchased the islands from Denmark. Built in the 1860s, the Government House serves as the administrative headquarters of the Virgin Islands, as well as the residence and office of the governor. It is furnished with antiques and paintings by Virgin Islands artist Camille Pissaro.

Territorial Name

Christopher Columbus named the islands *Las Virgenes* after St. Ursula and her followers. St. Ursula was the patron saint of British sailors.

Territorial Flower

The territorial flower of the U.S. Virgin Islands is the yellow elder, or yellow cedar, *Tecoma stans*, known by the local name Ginger Thomas. It was adopted by proclamation of Governor Paul Pearson in 1934.

Territorial Bird

The yellow breast, also called the sugar bird, is the territorial bird of the U.S. Virgin Islands.

Territorial Song

The territorial song of the U.S. Virgin Islands is "Virgin Islands March," with music by Alton A. Adams.

Population

The population of the U.S. Virgin Islands in 1990 was

The U.S. Virgin Islands consist of over 50 islands. Some are large, dotted with volcanic hills, reefs, and lagoons, and some are just rocks jutting out from the sea.

estimated to be 105,000. There are 789.5 persons per square mile—45.2 percent of the population live in towns and cities.

Geography and Climate

Located in the Caribbean Sea about 40 miles east of Puerto Rico, the U.S. Virgin Islands, consisting of three larger and 50 smaller islands, have a total area of 133 square miles. The climate is subtropical, with low humidity and an average temperature of 78 degrees. The islands are of volcanic origin and only the three largest are inhabited. The highest point, at 1,556 feet, is Crown Mountain on St. Thomas, and the lowest point is at sea level along the coasts. The chief ports are Cruz Bay on St. John, Frederiksted and Christiansted on St. Croix, and Charlotte Amalie on St. Thomas. St. Thomas is made up of a ridge of hills running east and west; St. Croix is hilly in the north, with flatlands and lagoons in the south; and St. John has steep lofty hills and valleys, with little level land.

Industries

The principal industries of the islands are tourism, aluminum ore refining, watch textiles, electronics, and petroleum refining. The chief manufactured products are rum, textiles, concrete, watch making, pharmaceuticals, scientific instruments, food products, aluminum products, and perfumes.

Agriculture

The chief crops of the islands are sugarcane, nuts, tomatoes, lettuce, mangoes, bananas, cucumbers, and spinach. Livestock is also important to the U.S. Virgin Islands; there are estimated to be 3,762 cattle, 2,889 sheep, 4,035 goats, and 18,345 chickens on its farms. Sand and gravel are important mineral resources.

Government

The U.S. Virgin Islands is an organized unincorporated territory. The governor and lieutenant governor are elected to four-year terms. The unicameral, or one-house, legislature consists of 15 members elected to two-year terms. The legislature begins its session in January and meets again several times during the year. The Revised Organic Act of 1954 serves as the territory's constitution. Virgin Islanders also elect a delegate to the U. S. House of Representatives for a two-year term. This delegate may vote in committee but not on the floor of the House. Although Virgin Islanders are citizens of the United States, they do not vote in national elections.

History

Prior to the arrival of the Europeans, the Virgin Islands were home to various tribes of Indians, including the Siboney, Arawak, and Carib.

Fort Christian in St. Thomas is one of the oldest standing structures in the Virgin Islands. Dating back to 1672, it once housed the entire St. Thomas colony.

The first European to reach the islands was Christopher Columbus, who landed on St. Croix in 1493, during his second trip to the New World. Although his landing party was driven away by the hostile Caribs, Columbus claimed the islands in the area for Spain. The Indians continued to fight off visitors until the mid-1500s, when King Charles I of Spain ordered his soldiers to kill the Indians and seize their land.

The Dutch, English, French, and Spanish explored the Virgin Islands in the 1600s, during which time it also served as a pirate base. It was not until 1672, however, that the first permanent European settlement was made by the Danes. Slaves were imported from Africa the following year to work on the sugar and cotton plantations.

By the early 18th century, the islands had been divided into two groups. British buccaneers took control of the eastern group—the British Virgin Islands—from the Dutch settlers. The islands remained part of the Leeward Islands Colony until 1956, when they became a separate dependency of Britain.

The western group of islands fell under the control of the Danes, and became known as a large slave market. The first hundred years of Danish rule saw the development of the islands controlled by the Danish West India and Guinea Company. The population of the area fell steadily with the decline of the sugar industry, and the United States expressed interest in acquiring the islands. It finally purchased them for $25 million in 1917 in order to prevent Germany from establishing military bases in the area. The purchase also gave the United States a base from which to safeguard the Panama Canal, which had been completed in 1914.

Virgin Islanders became citizens of the United States by a law passed in 1927. Following World War II, the U.S. put aside $10 million to fund projects to develop schools, hospitals, roads, and sewage and water systems in the islands. A new legislature was created in 1954, and Jon D. Merwin became the first native-born governor in 1958.

Today, the U.S. Virgin Islands enjoy a rapidly growing tourism industry.

Sports
Water sports dominate in the U.S. Virgin Islands. Sailing is extremely popular, as are surfing, deep-sea fishing, and diving.

Major Cities
Charlotte Amalie, St. Thomas (population 45,000). By the mid-1700s, Charlotte Amalie had been declared a free port. Because of this, it became the home base of

The Charlotte Amalie Harbor is the gateway to the island of St. Thomas and the most popular cruise port in the Caribbean.

traders and pirates such as Blackbeard and Captain Kidd. While under Danish rule, the town was a center of one of the largest slave trade operations in the world. The territorial capital of the U.S. Virgin Islands, Charlotte Amalie is the only town on the island of St. Thomas. The majority of people work for the government or in tourist-related industries.

Things to see in Charlotte Amalie: Blackbeard's Castle (1689), Bluebeard Castle, Government House (1867), Crown House (1750), St. Thomas Synagogue, the Dutch Reformed Church, Emancipation Park, Frederick Lutheran Church, Frenchtown, Grand Hotel (1841), Central Post Office, Hotel 1829 (1829), Legislative Building (1874), 99 Steps, Pissaro House, Fort Christian (1680), Market Square, New Herrnhut, and Royal Dane Mall.

Christiansted, St. Croix (population 22,500). The principal city of St. Croix, Christiansted briefly served as the capital of the Danish West Indies. The influence of the original Danish settlers can be seen in the city's numerous 18th-century building.
Things to see in Christiansted: Alexander Hamilton House (1750), Danish West India and Guinea Company Warehouse (1749), Fort Christiansvaern (1749), Government House (1747), Steeple Building, Old Danish Customs House (1734), and Scalehouse (1835).

Frederiksted, St. Croix (population 9,000). The emancipation of slaves on the islands was proclaimed at Fort Frederik on July 3, 1848. Thirty years later, much of the city was destroyed in a fire. Since then, it has been restored in Victorian style.
Things to see in Frederiksted: Apothecary Hall, Bellhouse, Customs House, Cruzan Rum Distillery, Judith's Fancy, Fort Frederik (1760), St. Patrick's Roman Catholic Church (1843), St. Paul's Episcopal Church (1812),

Christiansted is a beautiful harbor on the island of St. Croix, where a natural reef lies offshore, offering a haven for yachts and smaller boats.

The sugar mill at Whim Greathouse near Frederiksted is only part of the restored greathouse dating from the late 1700s.

Victoria House (1803), and the Old Danish School.

Places to Visit

The National Park Service maintains three areas in the U.S. Virgin Islands: Buck Island Reef National Monument and Christiansted National Historic Site on St. Croix, and Virgin Islands National Park on St. John.

Coki Point: Coral World. Visitors descend to the ocean floor in this underwater observatory, where they may see fish, coral formations, and deep-water flowers.

Near Frederiksted: St. George Village Botanical Garden. This 17-acre tropical garden contains ruins of a 19th-century rum factory and workers' village.

Whim Greathouse. Restored buildings include the main house, windmill, watch house and bathhouse, cookhouse and apothecary, museum, and gift shop.

The Annaberg Ruins on St. John are the remains of an 18th-century sugar plantation and mill.

Near Leinster Bay: Annaberg Plantation. The plantation includes the ruins of an 18th-century sugar estate and mill, which have been partially restored.

Near Magens Bay: Drake's Seat. Sir Francis Drake is said to have observed his fleet and watched for enemy ships from this point, which offers a panoramic view of the St. Thomas region.

Sugar Loaf Hill: Christ of the Caribbean. This statue, overlooking Hawksnest, Trunk, and Cinnamon bays, was built in 1953 by Colonel Julius Wadsworth with Terrance Powell.

Events

Sports: Horse racing at Flamboyant Park (St. Croix), Coral Bay Regatta (St. John), "Around St. John Race" (St. John), horse racing at Nadir Race Track (St. Thomas), Virgin Islands Open Blue Marlin Fishing Tournament (St. Thomas), Hook In & Hold On Boardsailing Regatta (St. Thomas), Little Switzerland Tennis Tournament (St. Thomas), International Rolex Cup Regatta (St. Thomas).

Arts and Crafts: Arts Festival (St. Croix), "Arts Alive!" (St.

Thomas).

Music: Caribbean Dance Company (St. Croix), Festival of the Arts (St. John), J'Ouvert Morning Tramp (St. Thomas).

Entertainment: Crucian Christmas Festival (St. Croix), Carnival (St. John), Carnival (St. Thomas), Market Square Food Festival (St. Thomas), Virgin Islands Charter Yacht Show (St. Thomas).

Tours: Atlantis Submarines (Charlotte Amalie), House Tours (St. Croix), Cruzan Rum Pavilion (St. Croix).

Theater: Island Center (St. Croix), Dorsch Cultural Center (St. Croix), Reichhold Center of the Performing Arts (St. Thomas).

Famous People

Many famous people were born in the U.S. Virgin Islands. Here are a few:

Sosthenes Behn 1882-1957, St. Thomas. Telephone corporation executive

Judah P. Benjamin 1811-64, St. Croix. Scholar, lawyer, and politician

Hugo Owen Bornn 1902-66, St. Thomas. Musician, composer, and educator

Judah P. Benjamin was one of the earliest Southern senators to advocate secession during the Civil War.

Almeris L. Christian b. 1919, St. Croix. U.S. federal court judge

Joe Christopher b. 1935, Frederiksted. Baseball player

Horace Clarke b. 1940, Frederiksted. Baseball player

Frank R. Crosswaith 1892-1965, St. Croix. Labor organizer

Jacob M. Da Costa 1833-1900, St. Thomas. Physician and educator

Melvin Evans b. 1917, Christiansted. First popularly elected governor of the U.S. Virgin Islands

Kelsey Grammer b. ?, St. Thomas. Television actor: *Cheers*

Emile Griffith b. 1938, St. Thomas. Welterweight and middleweight boxing champion

Ellie Hendricks b. 1940,

Camille Pissaro left the Virgin Islands at the age of 25 to become an impressionist painter in Paris. He was the only artist to exhibit in all eight impressionist shows.

Charlotte Amalie. Baseball player

Roy Innis b. 1934, St. Croix. Civil rights leader

David H. Jackson 1884-1946, St. Croix. Lawyer, politician, and labor organizer

Al McBean b. 1938, Charlotte Amalie. Baseball pitcher

Jose Morales b. 1944, Frederiksted. Baseball player

Camille Pissaro 1830-1903, St. Thomas. Artist

Terrance Todman b. 1926, St. Thomas. U.S. ambassador

Colleges and Universities
There is one university in the U.S. Virgin Islands. Listed is its location, date of founding, and enrollment. *University of the Virgin Islands*, Charlotte Amalie, St. Thomas, 1963, 2,665

Where To Get More Information
U.S. Virgin Islands Division of Tourism
1270 Avenue of the Americas
New York, NY 10020
1-212-582-4520

Guam

Windsurfing in Tumon Bay is a popular pastime for people who enjoy the outdoors.

Territorial Flag

The territorial flag of Guam, adopted in 1917, contains the great seal centered on a blue field. The flag is edged with a narrow red border and a wider white border.

Territorial Motto

Where America's Day Begins

The territorial motto of the island of Guam refers to its proximity to the international date line.

Tarague Beach, on the northern part of Guam, is one example of the beauty of the island.

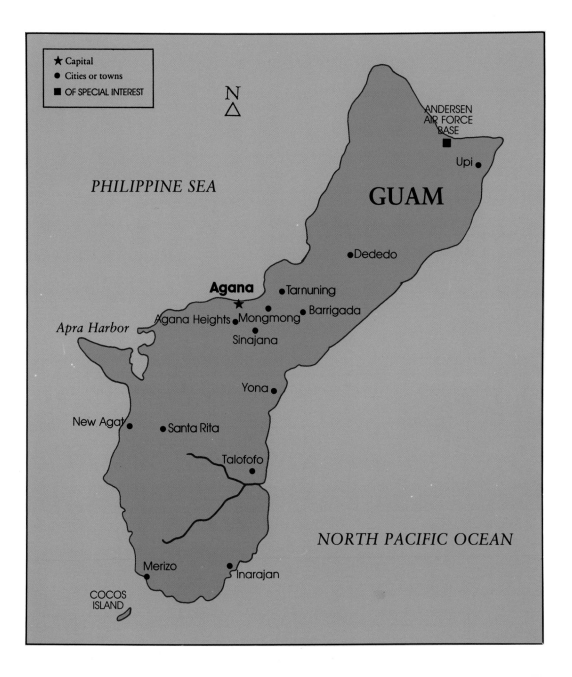

★ Capital
● Cities or towns
■ OF SPECIAL INTEREST

N
△

PHILIPPINE SEA

ANDERSEN
AIR FORCE
BASE
■

Upi ●

GUAM

●Dededo

Agana
★

●Tarnuning

Agana Heights ●Mongmong ●Barrigada

Sinajana

Apra Harbor

Yona ●

New Agat ● ● Santa Rita

Talofofo
●

NORTH PACIFIC OCEAN

Merizo ● ● Inarajan

COCOS
ISLAND

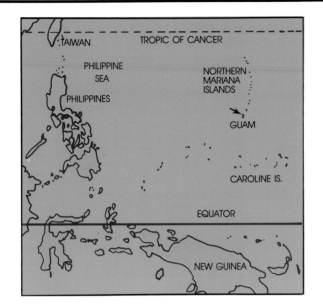

The governor of Guam lives in the Governor's House, which reflects the Spanish-style architecture on the island.

Territorial Capital

Agana is the territorial capital of Guam. This modern city has been rebuilt following its devastation in World War II.

Territorial Seal

The great seal of Guam depicts a coconut palm on the shore and a sailboat nearby on the water. The name "Guam" appears in red across the center of the seal.

Territorial Name

The name Guam comes from the word *guajan*, which means "we have" in the local dialect.

Territorial Flower

The puti tai nobio, or bougainvillea, is the territorial flower of Guam. This woody, tropical vine was named after Louis Antoine de Bougainville, a French explorer and scientist.

Territorial Tree

The ifit, or intsiabijuga, is the territorial tree of Guam.

This aerial view of southern Guam shows the geographic layout of the island.

Territorial Bird

The toto, or fruit dove, is the territorial bird of Guam.

Territorial Song

The territorial song of Guam is "Stand Ye Guamians."

Population

The population of Guam in 1990 was estimated to be 134,000. There are 641.1 persons per square mile— 39.5 percent of the population live in towns and cities.

Geography and Climate

Guam is the peak of a submerged mountain in the Marianas Trench. Located in the Pacific Ocean, 3,700 miles west of Hawaii, it has a total area of 209 square miles. The climate is tropical, with temperatures ranging from 70 to 90 degrees, and high humidity. Typhoons are common, and the average annual rainfall is about 90 inches. There are coral reefs off the coast of the island, a flat limestone plateau in the north, high cliffs along the ocean, and a volcanic mountain range in the south. The highest point, at 1,334 feet, is Mt. Lamlam in the southwest. There are several rivers on Guam, including the Ugum, Agana, Talofofo, and Pago. The chief port of the island is Apra Harbor.

Industries

The principal industries of the island are construction, petroleum refining, tourism, banking, and defense. The chief manufactured products are textiles, petroleum products, and foods.

Agriculture

The chief crops of the island are cabbages, eggplants, cucumbers, long beans, tomatoes, bananas, coconuts, watermelons, yams, cantaloupes, papayas, maize, and sweet potatoes. Livestock is also important in Guam; there are estimated to be 2,000 cattle and 14,000 hogs and pigs on its farms.

Government

Guam is a self-governing, organized, unincorporated territory of the United States, under the supervision of the Department of the Interior. The people of Guam elect a governor and lieutenant governor to four-year terms. The legislature consists of a unicameral, 21-member body elected every two years. The Organic Act of 1950 serves as the territory's constitution. Guamanians also elect a delegate to the U.S. House of Representatives. This delegate, who serves a two-year term, may vote in committee but not on the floor of the House. Guamanians are citizens of the United States but do not vote in national elections.

History

Archaeological evidence suggests that the first

This park was dedicated in 1977 to Chief Quipuha, who welcomed the first Jesuit missionaries to introduce Christianity in the Mariana Islands.

inhabitants of Guam arrived there about 3,000 years ago. The Chamorros, ancestors of today's Guamanians, are believed to have been the third group of people to live on the island before the Europeans arrived. They had an organized, complex culture, and lived in villages on the coast and near the rivers.

In 1521 the Portuguese explorer Ferdinand Magellan, discovered Guam, landing at Umatac Bay. It wasn't until 1565, however, that an expedition led by Miguel López de Legaspi formally claimed Guam, along with all of the Mariana Islands, for Spain. Over the next century, Guam served as a stopover for ships sailing between Mexico and the Philippines. Spanish missionaries established settlements on the island in 1688. At first, the Chamorros welcomed the Spaniards, but eventually they rebelled. During the

Two Lovers Point in Tumon Bay is a spot named for a young Chamorro couple whose love for each other was forbidden. According to legend, they tied their hair together and leapt to their death here.

years that followed, much of the native population was wiped out, in part due to fighting between Spain and the islanders, but more significantly because of diseases, such as smallpox, that were brought to the island by the Europeans.

The United States Navy occupied Guam in 1898, at the beginning of the Spanish-American War. When the war ended later that year, Spain ceded the island to the United States. Guam was placed under the administration of the U.S. Navy and became an important naval station. On December 8, 1941, Japan attacked the island, and the American forces surrendered two days later. Japan held Guam until 1944, when it was recaptured by the Americans.

In 1950, President Harry Truman signed an act giving Guam territorial status and making its people citizens of the United States. Joseph Flores, the first native Guamanian to serve as

The modern and majestic Pacific Star Hotel on Tumon Bay is just one of the many hotels that attracts visitors to Guam.

governor, was appointed in 1960. The first elected governor, Carlos G. Camacho, was inaugurated in 1971. In a referendum held in 1982, the people of Guam voted to become a commonwealth associated with the United States. Negotiations are currently under way.

Today, tourism is a rapidly expanding industry due to the large number of Japanese visitors to the island.

Sports

Water sports, including swimming, surfing, sailing, fishing, and scuba diving, are popular on Guam. Hunting for deer and boar is among the available activities, as are tennis, golf, and hiking. Cockfighting is an approved sport.

Major Cities

Agana (population 1,140). The capital city of Guam, Agana is located on the west coast of the island at the mouth of the Agana River. Bombs destroyed much of the city during World War II, but it has since been rebuilt. Agana has served as the seat of Guam's government under three flags—those of Spain, Japan, and the United States.
Things to see in Agana: Plaza de España, Kiosko, Azotea, Chocolate House, Tool Shed, Siesta Shed, Spanish Walls, Guam Museum, Dulce

The War in the Pacific National Historical Park at Ga'an Point in the village of Agat honors those who lost their lives in military conflicts in the area.

Nombre de María Cathedral (1669), and Santo Papa As Juan Pablo Dos Monument.

Places to Visit

The National Park Service maintains one area on Guam: War In The Pacific National Historical Park.

Apugan: Fort Santa Agueda. The fort, which dates from 1800, was constructed of burned limestones mixed with coral rocks.

Inarajan Village: Lanchon Antigo. This replica of a pre-20th century Chamorro village includes exhibits of local artifacts.

Kasamata Hill: Latte Park. Built around 500 A.D., these latte stoves—or house pillars—were moved to this location from Me'pu, an ancient Chamorro settlement.

Merizo: Merizo Conbento. Built in 1856, this is the island's oldest private residence still in use.

Tumon Bay: Padre San Vitores Shrine. The shrine is located at the site where Padre San Vitores, a Jesuit missionary, was killed.

Umatac: Fort Nuestra Señora de la Soledad. Built in the early 19th century, this fort overlooks Umatac Bay.

Yigo: South Pacific Memorial Park. Dominated by a tower symbolizing a praying figure, this park, which was dedicated in 1970, is a monument to the U.S. and Japanese determination for peace.

Events

Entertainment: Merizo Water Festival (Merizo Pier Park).

Famous People

Several famous people were born on Guam. Here is one:

Paul McDonald Calvo b. 1934, Agana. Governor of Guam

Colleges and Universities

There is one university in Guam. Listed is its location, date of founding, and enrollment.

University of Guam, Mangilao, 1952, 2,385

American Samoa

"April 17, 1900," the date of the first raising of the American flag over the territory, is printed on the top of the Territorial Seal of American Samoa. The *fue*, or fly switch, represents wisdom, while the to'oto'o, or staff, represents authority. The kava bowl symbolizes service to the chief, and the tapa cloth background represents the artistry of the Samoan people.

Territorial Flag
The territorial flag of American Samoa, adopted in 1960, consists of a blue field with a white triangle bordered in red pointing to the left. A white-headed eagle, which appears in the triangle, holds a yellow *uatogi*, or war club, representing the power of the state, and a *fue*, or fly switch, signifying wisdom.

Territorial Motto
Samoa Muamua le Atua
The territorial motto of American Samoa means, "In Samoa, God is first."

A breathtaking view of Fagaitus Village.

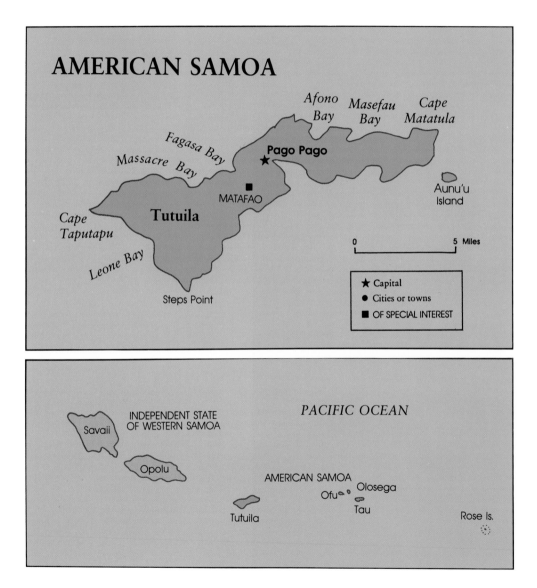

AMERICAN SAMOA

Afono Bay

Masefau Bay

Cape Matatula

Fagasa Bay

★ Pago Pago

Massacre Bay

Aunu'u Island

■ MATAFAO

Cape Taputapu

Tutuila

0   5 Miles

Leone Bay

Steps Point

★ Capital
● Cities or towns
■ OF SPECIAL INTEREST

PACIFIC OCEAN

INDEPENDENT STATE OF WESTERN SAMOA

Savaii

Opolu

AMERICAN SAMOA

Ofu   Olosega

Tau

Tutuila

Rose Is.

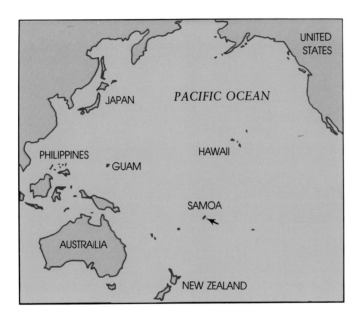

Population

The population of American Samoa in 1990 was estimated to be 39,700. There are 515.6 persons per square mile—17.5 percent of the population live in towns and cities.

Geography and Climate

Located in the southern central Pacific Ocean about 2,300 miles northeast of Hawaii, American Samoa has an area of 77 square miles. It consists of six small islands of the Samoan chain, including Tutuila, Aunu'u, Rose, and the Manu'a group—Ta'u, Olosega, and Ofu. Swain's Island, 210 miles to the northwest, is also administered as part of American Samoa. The climate is tropical, with an average rainfall of over 200 inches a year. Temperatures range from 70 to 90 degrees. The territory's highest point, at 3,050 feet, is Lata Mountain on the island of Tau, and the lowest point is at sea level along the coast. Rose and Swain's islands are made up

Territorial Capital

Pago Pago, on the island of Tutuila, is the territorial capital of American Samoa. The Government House is located in Fagatogo, the downtown area of the city.

Territorial Name

American Samoa was named after an ancient Pacific deity.

Territorial Flower

The territorial flower of American Samoa is the paogo, or ula-fala.

Territorial Plant

The ava is the territorial plant of American Samoa.

Territorial Song

The territorial song of American Samoa is "Amerika Samoa."

Baskets, carved wood objects, necklaces, and placemats are just a sampling of the handicrafts made and sold in Samoa.

of coral. The remaining islands are volcanic in origin, with mountainous terrain and some fertile land in the valleys. The chief port is Pago Pago, one of the best natural deep-water harbors in the Pacific.

Industries

The principal industries of the islands are tuna canning and tourism. The chief products are copra (dried coconut), handicrafts, and fish products.

Agriculture

The chief crops of the islands are taro, breadfruit, yams, coconuts, pineapples, oranges, and bananas. The only significant livestock is pigs. There are no important mineral resources.

Government

American Samoa is an unorganized, unincorporated territory of the United States, under the supervision of the Department of the Interior. The people elect a governor and lieutenant governor to four-year terms. Other department heads are appointed by the governor and lieutenant governor and approved by the legislature. The legislature consists of an 18-member senate and a 20-member house of representatives. In addition, one nonvoting delegate from Swain's Island is elected by the adult permanent residents. Senators, who are chosen by county councils, serve four-year terms, and representatives serve two-year terms. The most recent constitution was adopted in 1967. American Samoans elect a delegate to the U.S. House of Representatives who may vote in committee, but not on the floor of the House. American Samoans are nationals, but not citizens, of the United States. They do not vote in national elections.

History

Polynesians from eastern Melanesia arrived in Samoa about 2,000 years ago. The first European to see the islands was Jacob Roggeveen, a Dutch navigator. He sailed past without landing in 1722, and recorded the position of the islands inaccurately. As a result, forty years went by before Europeans visited the island again. In 1831, missionaries arrived and were welcomed by the islanders. American explorer Charles Wilkes surveyed the islands in 1839.

In 1878, the United States gained the rights to use Pago Pago harbor as a coaling station for the navy. Great Britain, Germany, and the United States signed an agreement in 1899 by which the Samoan Islands were divided between Germany and the U.S. Great Britain withdrew from the islands completely. In 1900, Germany took control of Western Samoa, and the United States took control of Tutuila,
Aunu'u, and Rose Island. The Manu'a group came under U.S. supervision in 1904, and Swain's Island was added in 1925. In 1951, the Department of the Interior took over the administration of the territory, which had previously been administered by the U.S. Navy.

In 1976, American Samoans approved a proposal allowing them the right to elect their own governor.
Two years later, the first popularly elected governor and lieutenant governor were inaugurated.

Today, tourism is a growing industry, and modern hotels, restaurants, and even a Mexican disco can be found on Tutuila.

Sports

Water sports such as swimming, diving, sailing, and fishing are extremely

Pago Pago Harbor was used as a coaling station for U.S. ships in the early 1900s and continues to service the U.S. Navy.

popular in American Samoa. The unofficial sport of the islands is *kirikiti*, which is a Polynesian version of cricket played with a hard rubber ball and a three-sided bat.

Major Cities
Pago Pago (population 3,400). Located on the island of Tutuila, Pago Pago is the capital city of American Samoa. Pago Pago Bay is the most spectacular deepwater port in the Pacific. There is a strong American influence which can be seen by the presence of the U.S. Navy, and the American goods for sale in the local supermarkets.
Things to see in Pago Pago:
Lyndon B. Johnson Tropical Medicine Center, Government House, and the Aerial Tramway at Mt. Alava.

Places to Visit
Aasu: Massacre Bay. The site of the massacre of Captain Jean François La Pérouse—a French scientist—and his eleven-member expedition in 1787 is marked by a monument erected by France in 1883.

Events
Arts and Crafts: The Samoan Village (Pago Pago).

Famous People
Several famous people were born in American Samoa. Here are two:
Tony Solaita 1947-90, Nuuyli. Baseball player
Jack Thompson b. 1956, Tutuila. Football quarterback

Colleges and Universities
There is one college in American Samoa. Listed is its location, date of founding, and enrollment.
American Samoa Community College, Pago Pago, 1970, 1,108

Where To Get More Information
Office of Tourism
American Samoan Government
Box 1147
Pago Pago, American Samoa 96799
(684) 699-9280

A young Samoan boy makes a colorful tapa print, one of the most popular crafts in Samoa.

Wake, Midway, and Other Islands

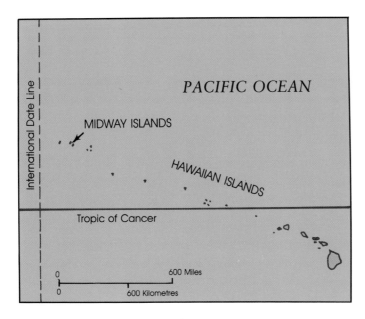

Hawaii; the Midway Islands, about 3 square miles, are 1,150 miles northwest of Hawaii; Johnston Atoll, 1 square mile, is 700 miles southwest of Hawaii; Palmyra Atoll, 4 square miles, is 1,000 miles south of Hawaii; Kingman Reef is 1,000 miles south of Hawaii; and Howland, Jarvis, and Baker islands are 1,500 to 1,650 miles southwest of Hawaii. Since these islands, with the exception of Midway, are located in the tropics, they are warm all year around, with an average temperature between 70 and 80 degrees. The Midway Islands are subtropical, with similar warm temperatures. Annual rainfall varies from island to island, with some receiving as much as 150 inches per year and others practically nothing.

Population

The population of Wake Island, together with its sister islands, Wilkes and Peale, consists of an estimated 300 United States Air Force personnel; the Midway Islands, Sand and Eastern, consist of an estimated 500 U.S. military personnel; Johnston Atoll consists of an estimated 1,000 U.S. government personnel and contractors; Kingman Reef, Palmyra Atoll (which is privately owned), and Howland, Jarvis, and Baker islands have been uninhabited since World War II.

Geography and Climate

Located in the central Pacific Ocean, Wake, Wilkes, and Peale islands occupy an area of less than 3 square miles and lie about 2,300 miles west of

Government

Each of the outlying territories in the Pacific has a civil government under the direct control of, or closely associated with, some federal

Wake Island was named for British Captain William Wake.

agency in Washington, D.C. Wake Island is an unincorporated territory of the United States and is administered by the U.S. Air Force; the Midway Islands are an unincorporated territory of the U.S. administered by the Department of the Navy; Johnston Atoll is an unincorporated territory of the U.S. operated by the Defense Nuclear Agency; Howland, Jarvis, and Baker islands are administered by the Department of the Interior; Palmyra Atoll is privately owned, and is administered by the Department of the Interior; and Kingman Reef is under Navy control. The Department of State is responsible for all affairs concerning islands in dispute.

History

Wake Island was probably first sighted by the Spanish explorer Alvaro de Mendaña around 1568. British Captain William Wake and his party were the first to land there, in 1796. An exploring expedition under Lieutenant Charles Wilkes surveyed the island in 1841. It was not until 1899, however, that Wake Island was formally claimed by the United States for use as a cable station. It was placed under naval jurisdiction in 1934 and became an air base the following year for traffic crossing the Pacific Ocean.

The Navy began construction of an air and submarine base on the island in 1941, shortly before the United States entered World War II. Due to its strategic position, the island came under attack from the Japanese on December 8 of that year, and was soon captured. The Japanese surrendered in 1945, and the base returned to U.S. control. The U.S. Air Force has administered the island since 1972.

The Midway Islands, originally called Middlebrooks and then Brooks, were discovered and claimed for the United States by Captain N. C. Brooks in 1859. They were annexed by the U.S. and given the name Midway eight years later. The islands came under the control of the Department of the Navy in 1903, and a cable relay station began operating there that same year.

Like Wake Island, Midway came under attack from the Japanese in 1941 due to its strategic position in the Pacific. However, Japan was not able to gain control of the island. In June of 1942, the turning point of the war occurred when the U.S. registered its first decisive victory over the Japanese at Midway.

The Midways today continue to be administered by the U.S. Department of the Navy.

Micronesia

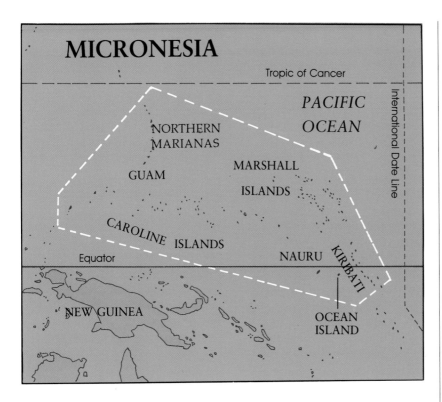

Territorial Flag

The territorial flag of Micronesia consists of four, white, five-pointed stars centered on a dark blue field.

Territorial Capitals

Saipan is the capital of the Commonwealth of the Northern Mariana Islands.

The capital of the Federated States of Micronesia is Palikir, on the island of Pohnpei. The United States has appropriated $15 million toward relocating the capital about 6 miles to the southwest, in the Palikir valley.

Majuro is the capital of the Republic of the Marshall Islands.

The capital of the Republic of Palau is Koror.

Territorial Name

The term *Micronesia,* meaning "little islands," is often used to refer to an area in the Pacific Ocean containing more than 2,100 islands. The three major archipelagoes—the Carolines, the Marshalls, and the Marianas—are separated into four political divisions. These are the Commonwealth of the Northern Mariana Islands, the Federated States of Micronesia, the Republic of the Marshall Islands, and the Republic of Palau.

Population

The population of the Commonwealth of the Northern Mariana Islands in 1990 was estimated to be 23,300. There are 126.6 persons per square mile—16.0 percent of the population live in towns and cities. Only six of the islands are inhabited.

The population of the Federated States of Micronesia in 1990 was estimated to be 108,000. There are 398.5 persons per square mile—19.4 percent of the population live in towns and cities.

The population of the Republic of the Marshall Islands in 1990 was estimated to be 45,600. There are 651.4 persons per square mile—47.8 percent of the population live in towns and cities.

The population of the Republic of Palau in 1990 was estimated to be 14,300. There are 80.8 persons per square mile—51.4 percent of the population live in towns and cities. Only eight of the islands are permanently inhabited.

Geography and Climate

The islands of Micronesia lie in the western central Pacific Ocean, between the Tropic of Cancer and the Equator. The Commonwealth of the Northern Mariana Islands consists of 16 islands with a total land area of 184 square miles. The total land area of the Federated States of Micronesia, which extends across the Caroline Island archipelago, is 271 square miles. The Republic of the Marshall Islands consists of two atoll chains comprised of 31 atolls, with a total land area of 70 square miles. The Republic of Palau consists of more than 200 islands in the Caroline chain, 8 of which are inhabited, with a total land area of 177 square miles. All of the islands of Micronesia are rugged mountains of volcanic origin, with the exception of the Marshall Islands, which are low coral atolls. The climate is tropical oceanic, with an average temperature of 80 degrees. Annual rainfall varies greatly, from only a few

inches per year in the low islands to an average of 150 inches annually in the high islands, especially the Carolines.

Industries

The principal industries of Micronesia are tourism and construction. The chief manufactured products are craft items made from shells, wood, and pearls.

Agriculture

The chief crops of Micronesia are coffee, coconuts, fruits, and tobacco from the Commonwealth of the Northern Mariana Islands; copra, black pepper, tropical fruits and vegetables, coconuts, cassavas, and sweet potatoes from the Federated States of Micronesia; coconuts, cacao, taro, breadfruit, fruits, and copra from the Republic of the Marshall Islands; and coconut, copra, cassavas, and sweet potatoes from the Republic of Palau. Most crops grown on the islands are for local consumption. The chief exported crop is copra, although vegetables are also exported from the Northern Marianas. Livestock is also important in Micronesia. Cattle and pigs are raised in the Northern Mariana Islands; pigs, cattle, and goats in the Marshall Islands; and pigs and chickens in the Federated States of Micronesia. Deep seabed minerals, marine products, and forests are important natural resources. In addition, there are phosphate deposits in the Marshall Islands and gold in Palau. Commercial fishing is a minor economic activity in Palau and the Marshall Islands.

Government

From 1947 to 1986, Micronesia was known as the United States Trust Territory of the Pacific Islands. In 1986, the trusteeship was dissolved and the Federated States of Micronesia, the Republic of the Marshall Islands, and the Republic of Palau signed a Compact of Free Association with the United States. At the same time, the Northern Mariana Islands became a commonwealth of the U.S. Because Palauans did not approve the Compact, their republic is still administered by the trusteeship.

Each of the four political divisions of Micronesia is self-governing. The people of the Commonwealth of the Northern Mariana Islands elect a governor and lieutenant governor. The legislature consists of a nine-member senate and a 15-member house of representatives. Senators serve four-year terms and representatives serve two-year terms. The most recent constitution was adopted in 1978. The people of the Northern Marianas are citizens of the United States, but do not vote in national elections.

The president and vice-president of the Federated States of Micronesia are elected from among the members of the National Congress of the Federated States of Micronesia, which is the legislative body of the territory. The legislature is unicameral, and its senators are elected by the people. The most recent constitution was adopted in 1979. Each of the four states of the territory—Ponape, Yap, Truk, and Kosrae—elects its own legislature and governor.

The president of the Republic of the Marshall Islands is elected by a 33-member, unicameral parliament, or *Nitijela*. He appoints a Cabinet of Ministers. A Council of *Iroij*, or chiefs, serves as a consultative body on matters involving traditional law and custom. The most recent constitution was adopted in 1979.

The president and vice-president of the Republic of Palau are elected by the people. A Council of Chiefs advises the president on matters of traditional law and customs. The legislature of Palau consists of a house of delegates and a senate. The most recent constitution went into effect in 1980.

History

The first inhabitants of Micronesia came from Indonesia and the Philippines about 1500 B.C. In 1521, the Portuguese explorer Ferdinand Magellan discovered the islands of Guam, Saipan, and Rota in the Northern Marianas while sailing westward across the Pacific Ocean. Spain formally took possession of the islands following the voyage of Miguel López de Legaspi in 1565. The Carolines were also claimed by Spain at that time. In 1592, Spain took possession of the Marshall Islands. These two groups were largely undisturbed until the late 19th century, when Germany took over the administration of Jaluit and Ebon in the Marshall Islands.

In 1898, at the end of the Spanish-American War, Spain sold the Caroline and Northern Mariana islands, excluding Guam, to Germany.

Yap stone was the traditional currency of the island. As the huge stones were too large to move, the title, or ownership, of the stones would be exchanged for goods or services.

The Germans increased the production of copra, introduced phosphate mining, and improved sanitation, education, and roads.

Shortly after the start of World War I, Japan captured Palau and the Marshall Islands. Following the war, the League of Nations mandated the Northern Mariana, Caroline, and Marshall islands to Japan. During the Japanese period, roads, docks, and water systems were built, and

mining, agriculture, fishing, and sugar-processing industries were developed. Japan held the islands until 1944, when American forces captured many Japanese installations in Micronesia. The islands were placed under the administration of the U.S. Navy until 1947, when the United Nations established the Trust Territory of the Pacific Islands. The U.S. Navy continued to administer the territory until 1951, at which time the supervision was transferred to the Department of the Interior.

In 1975, the Northern Mariana Islands approved the Covenant to Establish a Commonwealth. By 1978, a constitution went into effect, and the United States officially recognized the territory as an independent commonwealth, although the arrangement did not become completely legal until the United Nations' trusteeship was dissolved in 1986.

The Marshall Islands, Palau, Truk, Yap, Ponape, and

Kosrae also negotiated with the United States for independence. The constitution of the Republic of the Marshall Islands took effect on May 1, 1979. Truk, Yap, Ponape, and Kosrae joined together under the name Federated States of Micronesia. Its constitution went into effect on May 10, 1979. Palau began operating under its own constitution in 1981. All three territories signed the Compact of Free Association in 1982. The Compact provides that the United States recognizes the three former Trust Territory dependencies as separate states and accepts responsibility for their defense. The United States also agreed to provide economic aid in return for permission to continue its military operations in the islands. In 1986, voters in the Federated States of Micronesia and the Republic of the Marshall Islands approved the Compact and entered into free association with the United

States. As of 1990, voters in the Republic of Palau had not yet approved it. As a result, Palau is technically still under the trusteeship.

Today, tourism has become a major industry in Micronesia. In an agreement with the Commonwealth of the Northern Mariana Islands, the United States has pledged $228 million until 1992 for capital improvements, government operations, and special programs.

Major Cities
Palikir, Federated States of Micronesia (population 5,549). Palikir is the capital and largest city of the Federated States of Micronesia.
Koror, Republic of Palau (population 9,442). Koror is the capital and largest city of the Republic of Palau.
Majuro, Marshall Islands (population 14,267). The capital and largest city of the Marshall Islands, Majuro is a large atoll, with many of its islands connected by roads.

The city is the administrative center of the islands and offers excellent swimming at many of its beaches.
Saipan, Northern Mariana Islands (population 19,442). The capital and largest city of the Northern Mariana Islands, Saipan is a busy commercial center. The remains of several American airfields built during World War II may still be seen.
Things to see in Saipan: Suicide Cliff, the old Japanese jail, the last Japanese command post, the old Japanese hospital, Peace Memorial, Sugar King monument, blue grotto, and Bird Island.

Colleges and Universities
The College of Micronesia is the only institute of higher education in Micronesia. The three campuses of the college are the School of Nursing on Saipan, Community College of Micronesia on Ponape, and the Micronesian Occupational College on Palau.

Bibliography

General

Howe, K.R. *Where the Waves Fall: A New South Sea Island History from First Settlement to Colonial Rule.* 1984.

Puerto Rico

Colorado, Antonio J. *The First Book of Puerto Rico*, 2nd ed. New York: Franklin Watts, 1972.

McKown, Robin. *The Image of Puerto Rico: Its History and Its People, One the Island—One the Mainland.* New York: McGraw-Hill, 1973.

Perl, Lila. *Puerto Rico: Island Between Two Worlds.* New York: William Morrow, 1979.

Singer, Julia. *We All Come from Someplace: Children of Puerto Rico.* New York: Atheneum, 1976.

Steiner, Stanley. *The Islands: The Worlds of the Puerto Ricans.* New York: Harper & Row, 1974.

United States Virgin Islands

Creque, Darwin D. *The U.S. Virgins and the Eastern Caribbean.* Whitmore, 1968.

Eggleston, George T., *Virgin Islands.* Melbourne, FL: Krieger, 1973.

Moore, James E. *Everybody's Virgin Islands.* New York: Lippincott, 1979.

Tansill, Charles C. *The Purchase of the Danish West Indies.* Westport, CT: Greenwood Press, 1968.

Guam

Carano, Paul, and Pedro C. Sanchez. *A Complete History of Guam.* Rutland, VT: Tuttle, 1964.

Farrell, Don A. *Guam: 1898-1918.* Micronesian, 1985.

Ishikawa, Wes. *The Elder Guamanians.* Campile, 1977.

Lutz, William. *Guam.* 1987.

Thompson, Laura. *Guam and Its People*, 3rd rev. ed. 1969.

American Samoa

Henry, Fred. *Samoa, an Early History.* 1980.

Micronesia

Alkire, William H. *An Introduction to the Peoples and Cultures of Micronesia*, 2nd ed. 1977.

Brower, Kenneth. *Micronesia: The Land, the People and the Sea.* Baton Rouge: Louisiana State University Press, 1982.

Hughes, Daniel T., and Sherwood G. Lingenfelter. *Political Development in Micronesia.* Columbus: Ohio State University Press, 1974.

Nevin, David. *The American Touch in Micronesia.* New York: Norton, 1977.

Photo Credits/Acknowledgments

Photos on pages 3 (top), 5, 6-7, 9, 10, 12, 14, 15, 16, 17, 18, 19, courtesy of Puerto Rico Travel Commission; pages 3 (bottom), 23, 24-25, 27, 28, 30, 31, 32, 33, 34, courtesy of U.S. Virgin Islands Division of Tourism; pages 37, 38-39, 41, 42, 43, 44, 45, 46, courtesy of Guam Visitors Bureau; pages 4, 47, 48-49, 52, 53, 54, courtesy of American Samoa Government Office of Tourism; page 60, courtesy of Embassy of the Federated States of Micronesia (Dick Merritt); pages 20, 21, 34, 35, 56, courtesy of New York Public Library.

Cover photograph courtesy of Puerto Rico Travel Commission.